T0022126

THE ANIMALS OF THE FROZEN NORTH

An Arctic Story

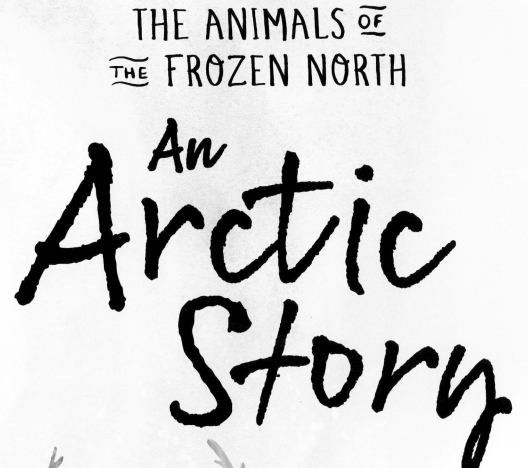

For all the animals of the Arctic. And in memory of Barry Lopez,
with thanks for his marvelous book, *Arctic Dreams* —J. B.
For Isaac—K. B.

A Raspberry Book
Art direction & design: Sidonie Beresford-Browne
Design: Ailsa Cullen and Andy Bowden
Text: Jane Burnard
Illustration: Kendra Binney
Consultant: Paul Lawston

KINGFISHER
LONDON & NEW YORK

Text and design copyright © Raspberry Books Ltd 2022
First published 2022 in the United States by Kingfisher,
120 Broadway, New York, NY 10271
Kingfisher is an imprint of
Macmillan Children's Books, London
All rights reserved

Distributed in the U.S. and Canada by Macmillan,
120 Broadway, New York, NY 10271

EU representative: 1st Floor, The Liffey Trust Centre,
117-126 Sheriff Street Upper, Dublin 1 D01 YC43

Library of Congress Cataloging-in-Publication Data has been applied for.

ISBN 978-0-7534-7846-2

Kingfisher books are available for special promotions and premiums.
For details contact: Special Markets Department, Macmillan, 120 Broadway,
New York, NY 10271

For more information, please visit
www.kingfisherbooks.com

Printed in China
1 3 5 7 9 8 6 4 2
1TR/0622/RV/WKT/140MA

THE ANIMALS OF THE FROZEN NORTH

An Arctic Story

WRITTEN BY
JANE BURNARD

ILLUSTRATED BY
KENDRA BINNEY

KINGFISHER
LONDON & NEW YORK

ARCTIC WOLF

SNOWY OWL

WOOD FROG

NORTH POLE

LEMMING

CARIBOU

WALRUS

MUSK OXEN

POLAR BEAR

SNOW GEESE

This is the ARCTIC.

It sits on the top of the world—
a frozen sea in a circle of land.

It is cold, vast, and full of animals.

They are made for this place,
and it is made for them.

ARCTIC FOX

NARWHAL

BELUGA WHALE

ARCTIC HARE

Dark, thick forests full of needles and cones edge the Arctic. Mosses, lichens, and mushrooms cover the ground. Among the pools and lakes of the forest lives a delicate little creature:

THE WOOD FROG.

Winter is coming to the Arctic.

Excited calls come from the clean blue sky. A wobbling "V" of bright white snow geese flaps high and fast over the treetops, traveling south.

LICHEN

MOSS

MUSHROOM

Snow falls softly.

The pools and lakes freeze over.
The wood frog burrows into the forest floor.
She crouches there as snow piles up like a
blanket to cover her. Then she freezes, from the
outside in, until even her tiny heart is encased
in ice. Her eyes glaze over. She's as solid as
a smooth, round pebble. There is no more
movement, no more heartbeat,
no more breathing.

But yet she's alive.

WOOD FROGS can survive being frozen solid for seven months
of the year. They produce a sugar called glucose in their bodies,
which allows them to freeze but stops them from being damaged
and drying out. They stay frozen throughout the harsh Arctic
winter, in temperatures as low as -50°F (-45°C).

At the edge of the forest, trees thin out
and grow shorter and shorter, until they hug
the ground in patches like mats. This is the
tundra—a flat, rocky plain divided by rivers,
swept now by freezing winter winds. The soil
here is thin and poor, and just beneath the
surface lies ice that never melts.

Plants that grow
here are tough and small.
SO IS THIS LEMMING.

On the horizon to the north, a huge, gray
shape is moving across the ground,
heading for the timberline through fast-falling snow.
It is a herd of caribou, thousands and thousands of animals,
their coats the color of shining new moons. They surge
through rivers, splashing in sparkling, icy water. As they
grow closer, the lemming squeaks and dives for the
safety of his burrow.

These are BARREN-GROUND CARIBOU, which make
the longest migrations of any land animal,
covering over 600 mi. (1,000 km) a year. In the fall
they move south to shelter at the edge of forests.
Here they find lichens and mosses, the plants
that make up their winter food.

This busy little creature is ready for winter. He's found shelter under the tundra's snow and ice, burrowing long tunnels that lead to a cozy, grass-lined nest. From here he darts around undercover, digging to find grasses and twigs to eat.

As winter sets in,

the Arctic breathes out an icy breath and the weak daytime sun circles lower and lower on the southern horizon. Some animals, like snow geese and caribou, travel to warmer places, where there is more food. But the lemming stays put on the frozen tundra.

But above him, on a rocky, windswept mound, a snowy owl turns her head. Her sharp ears have picked up the sound of the lemming's tiny scamperings. Lifting soundlessly from her perch, she drops swiftly and pounces, claws first, on the powdery snow . . .

and misses him.

Spreading her huge wings,
the snowy owl flaps and takes to the air,
feathered feet dangling for a moment,
spilling snow, before tucking into her
body as she soars away.

*From high above
the tundra*
her farsighted, yolk-yellow eyes
search the white world below for
any sign of movement. She sees
the Sun, now a golden line on the
horizon to the south.

She sees an **ARCTIC FOX**,
trotting into the wind. She sees a line
of hungry **POLAR BEARS**, prowling
the coast to the north, waiting for
sea ice to form.

But even she misses the **ARCTIC HARE**,
crouching, eyes narrowed against the wind,
still against the cover of a rock.

The air is so
cold and clear
you can see the owl's
breath, trailing behind
her as she flies.

SNOWY OWLS are the only birds of prey to live in the Arctic all year
round. But because Arctic winters are so cold and prey so scarce,
only very experienced, adult snowy owls can hunt here successfully
in the winter. Their white coloring camouflages them among the
snow and ice, and their velvety feathers help them fly soundlessly.

This is the edge of the tundra

—the place where Arctic land meets Arctic sea. This far north, the sky holds on to the colors of dawn and dusk for hours. The Sun hardly rises at all. It surfaces in the south, hangs like a golden ball in the sky, then disappears just two hours later.

Like the polar bears, the small, neat **ARCTIC FOX** is waiting for the sea to freeze over.

Already the water looks like thick, dark oil, rippling slowly under an icy skin. Larger pieces of ice are forming into flat, gray chunks.

But the sea's not solid yet.

ARCTIC FOXES' thick, snow-white winter coats are among the warmest in the world, and their fluffy tails act as blankets when they curl up to sleep. Like the snowy owl, they rely on lemmings for food. Any they can't eat they bury in neat rows underground, for when food is scarce.

The fox stops dead in his tracks.

Slowly, soundlessly, he moves
his head from side to side,
listening carefully.

Then, suddenly,
he leaps high in
the air . . .

. . . and
plunges
down, head
first, into
snow.

This lemming isn't so lucky.

The Sun has abandoned the Arctic now.

In the icy temperatures, the sea has frozen thick
and solid. In this twilight world there is no liquid water,
no land—only an endless desert of ice and snow.

In a snowdrift under the shelter of a cliff,
a female **POLAR BEAR** sighs and settles in her cozy den.

Her cubs are days old—as small as squirrels, blind, deaf,
and helpless. She will nurse them here all winter.

POLAR BEAR cubs are usually born in December, when temperatures remain as
low as -40°F (-40°C) for long periods. By using their own body heat—and by
adjusting the air flow into the den and the thickness of its snow walls—mother
bears keep their dens at a constant temperature of about 32°F (0°C).

But a male polar bear

prowls swiftly north to where it's darkest and coldest.
Long neck stretched forward, white coat shimmering
around powerful limbs, he's searching for seals.

Behind him, at a safe distance,
bounces the crafty arctic fox—he knows
that where there are polar bears there
is leftover meat.

Further out to sea, the ice shifts slowly, pushed by currents and scoured by winds. As it warps and crunches together, it moans and wails, then—**CRACK!**—it splits apart, revealing a channel of black water.

The **BEAR** stops suddenly.

His head tilts and his small ears swivel. Carefully, he sniffs the icy air.

INSIDE THE BREATHING HOLE

From deep below the ice, a ringed seal swims up and into the cone-shaped breathing hole that she made herself with the claws of her front flippers.

The circular patterns on her smooth, sleek skin look like the craters on the full Moon.

Over the roaring wind the bear hears a tiny swish and a tinkle of droplets: the ringed seal, hauling herself out to rest inside her snow lair.

The hair between the bear's wide footpads muffles the **CRUNCH** of snow as he creeps forward. Then he lunges, slamming powerfully through the roof.

But not before the **SEAL** slithers back into her breathing hole and swims away to safety under the ice.

RINGED SEALS burrow up into the snow above their breathing holes to make "snow lairs"—snug shelters where they hide from predators. They find fish and small crustaceans, such as shrimp, to eat beneath the ice, even in the darkness of winter.

Soaring hundreds of miles

into the sky, a curtain of soft greens and pinks billows gently, weightlessly. Beneath it, sea ice floats in a jumble of pieces, large and small. Towering icebergs drift, driven by underwater currents.

AURORA BOREALIS

NARWHALS sleep on the surface of the ocean, spouting water as they slowly breathe out. From time to time they raise their sensitive tusks above the water, as if to sniff the air.

NARWHALS

The AURORA BOREALIS happens when tiny particles stream out from the Sun and meet Earth's atmosphere, producing energy that makes moving colors appear in polar skies at night. The lights sometimes make sounds: swishes, rustles, hisses, and pops!

BELUGA WHALES glide ghostlike beneath thin sheets of ice in great herds. They keep their young, who are small and gray, safe among them.

Sound fills the still water and sky.

The curtain of colored light swishes above. Narwhals buzz and crackle in their sleep. Belugas click and whistle. And walruses bellow contentedly.

WALRUSES sprawl on a large piece of ice—a shifting, brown island, dotted with pairs of bright white tusks.

BELUGA WHALES

NARWHALS and BELUGA WHALES have thick layers of blubber to keep them warm in freezing water. Unlike most whales, they have no dorsal fins, which would cause heat loss and make swimming under ice difficult. The male narwhal's spiraled tusk is an overgrown tooth, full of nerve endings. Belugas' white coloring helps them blend in to seas full of ice.

After four months of Arctic darkness,
the Sun has spun a brief, golden line on
the southern horizon.

Slowly, very slowly,
the solid ice begins to break
apart and melt.

By a long bank of shore ice, belugas gather and move apart.

Some dive to scour the
ocean floor for **SHRIMP**,
some herd fish for others
to catch, some chase
each other for fun.

And a single walrus—
a great, weathered male with
gleaming tusks and luminous
whiskers—lies on the ice after
feasting on clams.

A pack of **WOLVES** has
many mouths to feed and is always
looking for prey, always on the move.
The wolves have spotted the walrus.
They know it is too big for them,
but they are hungry.

They charge.

WALRUSES can weigh up to
1.5 tons. They use their huge
tusks to pull themselves out
of the sea and on to ice. Their
wrinkled skin can measure
4 in. (10 cm) thick, which,
together with a thick layer of
blubber, keeps them warm in
freezing Arctic temperatures.

The **WALRUS** knows he is too big
for them too, but he lunges forward
anyway. His great bulk crashes through
the ice and he speeds away,

*swift and sinuous
in water.*

It is almost spring,
and the Sun hangs uncertainly
above the tundra's horizon.

But a **BLIZZARD** blows wildly,
almost blotting it out.

A herd of musk oxen drift in single file through the
snow. They are hungry, heading for better grazing on
higher ground, where the snow is thinner.

But the **WOLVES** are
back, and they're hungry
too. Suddenly, light-footed
female wolves spring ahead
of the oxen, darting back
and forth.

Long, glossy hair swirls

as the oxen turn and come together, but behind them are powerful male wolves, crouching, teeth bared, ready to **POUNCE**.

As one, the oxen shift to form a defensive ring, standing shoulder to shoulder, flank to flank, their long hooked horns and large brown eyes facing the wolves.

They keep their young tight within the ring. The wolf pack are testing their prey, watching for weakness.Though the wolves circle, the oxen's formation holds.

THERE IS NO WAY IN.

Unlike other types of wolves, almost all ARCTIC WOLVES are white. They live in family packs and are fiercely loyal to the pack and their leader. They aren't the biggest or the fastest predators in the Arctic, but their intelligence and teamwork make them very successful hunters.

The wolves' leader howls a signal and the pack backs off,

for now.

As spring arrives,

the Sun lifts higher and higher in the south.

~

Ice and snow melt, filling the tundra's fast-flowing rivers with cold, clean water. The Arctic is breathing a warm breath in, welcoming back the **CARIBOU**, who will spend their summer here.

Sunlight shimmers

on the **MUSK OXEN'S** long coats as they paw the melting snow to uncover their food:

mosses,   roots,

and lichens.

Suddenly playful, young oxen race around and kick up their heels.

In the snowdrift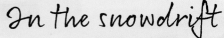
under the shelter of a cliff,
the female **POLAR BEAR**
punches out a hole in
the snow,

As the family of bears claw their
way out and slide down the snowy
slope, the cubs make small cries—
timid and excited all at once.

letting **SUNLIGHT** and the
sounds and smells of the **TUNDRA**
pour into her den.

Except for POLAR BEARS, MUSK OXEN are
the largest animals to live on the tundra.
They have two layers of fur to keep them
warm in winter—a dense underfur of fine,
woolly hairs, then a thick covering of "guard
hair," which can grow as long as 2 ft. (60 cm).

At the southern edge of the tundra,

trees grow thicker and taller, until their wide trunks and needled branches make a dense, dark forest.

As the Sun shines warmly on the treetops, something stirs beneath the leaf litter at their roots. The **WOOD FROG** is thawing from the inside out.

Her tiny heart begins to beat again. Her muscles soften and twitch, her eyes clear. She blinks. Then she hops away. There's a lot to do. She must find a mate and a pond in which to lay her eggs.

Huge, honking flocks of **SNOW GEESE** flap high and fast through the sun-filled sky. In wild, white flurries of birds they're heading north, returning to the place where their own eggs hatched, to breed again . . .

. . . returning to the tundra, which the brief Arctic summer will coat in bursts of **WILDFLOWERS**.

Traveling high in the sky at speeds of up to 70 mi. (110 km) per hour, millions of SNOW GEESE fly almost 3,000 mi. (5,000 km) north to breed on the tundra after spending the winter in southern coastal marshes, bays, wet grasslands, and fields. Pairs mate for life, nesting on the ground in large, noisy colonies, which give some protection against predators such as arctic foxes.

This is the Arctic.

It sits on the top of the world—
a frozen sea in a circle of land.

It is cold, vast, and full of animals.

They are made for this place,
and it is made for them.